The Nature of Things Fragile

The Nature of Things Fragile

POEMS

Peter Vertacnik

WINNER OF THE NEW CRITERION POETRY PRIZE

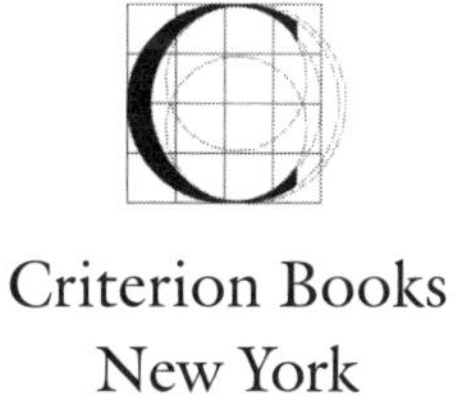

Criterion Books

New York

First American edition published in 2024 by Criterion Books, an imprint of Encounter Books, an activity of Encounter for Culture and Education, Inc., a nonprofit, tax-exempt corporation.

www.newcriterion.com/poetryprize
www.encounterbooks.com

Manufactured in the United States and printed on acid-free paper. The paper used in this publication meets the minimum requirements of ANSI/ NISO Z39.48–1992 (R 1997) (Permanence of Paper).

LIBRARY OF CONGRESS CATALOGING-IN-PUBLICATION DATA IS AVAILABLE

Information for this title can be found at the Library of Congress website under ISBN 9781641773652 and LCCN 2023038198.

Contents

I

Art   3

Bedtime Story   4

Visiting Hours   5

Juke   6

Departure   8

Balance   10

Reading Together   11

The Quality of Small   12

Face Value   13

Caught   14

Home Movies   16

Photograph   18

The Diver   19

False Elegy Beginning with the Moon   20

Odd Elegy   22

Sleeping in Your Parents' Bed   23

Lullaby for an Adult   24

Apology to Candles   25

Late Inquiry   26

II

Dial Tone	31
In Memory of Ray Dolby	32
Wind	33
Hyperopia	34
Deciduous	35
Seasonal	36
Standardized	37
Malpractice	38
Patient	39
Prognosis	40
Fears	41
Vanity	42
Teacher's Lament	43
The Viewer	44
Collars	45
My Mama's Schmaltz	46

III

Early June, Mid-Michigan	51
In Praise of Blank Cassettes	52

Ground Level   54

The Yellowjackets Speak   55

Peonies in July   56

The Two-Body Problem in Cyberspace   57

Anesthetic   58

Mourning Doves   60

Winter Palette   62

Trace   63

Sugar Beets   64

Stumbling   66

Gardeners   67

The Fenced Field   68

Constitutional   69

After   70

The Book   71

Gray Areas   72

The Question   73

Daybreak on Lake Huron   74

Endnotes   77

Acknowledgments

Grateful acknowledgment is made to the editors of the following publications in which these poems previously appeared, often in slightly different forms:

8 Poems: "Constitutional"
32 Poems: "Trace"
Alabama Literary Review: "Collars," "My Mama's Schmaltz" & "Teacher's Lament"
The American Journal of Poetry: "Reading Together"
The Asses of Parnassus: "Deciduous" (as "Riddle"), "Dial Tone," "Hyperopia," "Malpractice," "Patient," "Prognosis" (as "Final Illness") & "Standardized"
Autumn Sky Poetry Daily: "In Praise of Blank Cassettes" & "Visiting Hours" (reprint)
Bad Lilies: "The Diver," "Seasonal" & "The Yellowjackets Speak"
Better Than Starbucks: "Fears"
Clackamas Literary Review: "Departure" & "The Question"
The Cortland Review: "Odd Elegy"
Folio: "Mourning Doves"
Hampden-Sydney Poetry Review: "The Quality of Small"
The Hopkins Review: "Anesthetic" & "Apology to Candles"
Literary Matters: "False Elegy Beginning with the Moon" & "The Viewer"
Lucid Rhythms: "Art" & "Visiting Hours"
The MacGuffin: "Face Value" (as "My Father's Face")
The Midwest Quarterly: "The Fenced Field"
The New Criterion: "Late Inquiry"
North Dakota Quarterly: "After" & "Wind"
The Orchards Poetry Journal: "Bedtime Story"
Pembroke Magazine: "Gardeners"
Phoebe: "Lullaby for an Adult"
Poet Lore: "Balance"
Potomac Review: "Ground Level"
Psaltery & Lyre: "Sugar Beets"
Rat's Ass Review: "Vanity"
River Heron Review: "Daybreak on Lake Huron"

South Florida Poetry Journal: "Home Movies"
THINK: "Sleeping in Your Parents' Bed"
Valparaiso Poetry Review: "Peonies in July"
Water~Stone Review: "The Book"

"Daybreak on Lake Huron" was the winner of the 2019 Texas Association of Creative Writing Teachers Graduate Student Prize in Poetry.

Many thanks are due to professors Curtis Bauer, Terry Harpold, Michael Hofmann, Jacqueline Kolosov, William Logan, Brian McFadden, Ange Mlinko, and William Wenthe, as well as my classmates and students at Texas Tech University and The University of Florida.

I'd also like to recognize those who have supported my writing at different times over the years as teachers, mentors, correspondents, collaborators, colleagues, and friends, especially Arthur Athanason, Brian Brodeur, William Brown, Patrick Cheney, Boris Dralyuk, Lupita Eyde-Tucker, Gordon Henry, Ernest Hilbert, Laura Knoppers, Taylor Light, Joshua Mehigan, Alexis Sears, Matthew Buckley Smith, Carmine Starnino, Timothy Steele, Adam Tavel, Mary Ellen Vaydik, Diane Wakoski, David Yezzi, Yifan Zhang, and Jane Zwart.

Finally, my gratitude belongs always with Kim Vertacnik (my self-proclaimed "last and worst reader") for years of abiding humor, encouragement, and love, whether near or far.

for my family

That soughing at the sill—
Is it a requiem for the fisted spider,
His harvest a tall crown

Of iridescent ruins, of tiny shipwrecks:
The nature of things fragile
Made manifest?

—Henri Coulette

The Nature of Things Fragile

I

The night, the night alone is old
And showed me only what I knew,
Knew, yet never had been told;
A speech that from the darkness grew
Too deep for daily tongues to say,
Archaic dialogue of a few
Upon the sixth or the seventh day.

—Edwin Muir

Art

In her rote monotone our teacher said,
"Now draw your family." A common task
for Art, until a classmate thought to ask
could we include them all, alive and dead?

"Um . . . yes." Later, though, when she paused beside
my desk, examining what I had drawn,
that his crib was no crib refused to dawn
on her. "How old's your brother?" "One," I lied.

Bedtime Story

Your story was the first our mother told me
that I can still recall once having heard.
If there were others earlier, they've since
been covered over, paper layers pasted
on aging walls, inaccessible

but present, which is how I think of you—
not as my angel or a guardian,
though she insisted often. Even back then,
as a child frightened by darkness, it seemed wrong
to say you had been taken for a purpose,

however much it helped me sleep. And yet
I can't help turning back to that staged tale
if for no other purpose than brief comfort,
surely one reason why our mother kept
repeating it, more for herself than me.

I don't remember when she stopped, when I
began to *think* it to myself each night:
just as a child who's learned to read forgets
that day when syllables, once mouthed aloud,
transposed themselves beyond the audible.

Visiting Hours

That evening while her loved ones sat beside
the bed it seemed she might be getting well.
Even when her boy fidgeted and cried
she felt calm, lulled by his familiar smell,

as by her husband's voice when he recounted
his day: a haircut, work, the grocery store.
Both scent and tenor gradually surmounted
the fear that she should never hope for more

than intermittent health. No regimen
or drug the doctors ordered could relieve
the pain her family had quelled again
by visiting, though soon they'd have to leave.

Then she would wait alone for sleep, a guest
who seldom came; or coming, brought no rest.

Jake

The young boy learns
his stuffed bear's name
a short time after
he learns his own.

He has arrived belatedly
to a worn world,
a place where litter
and bootprints blotch sidewalks

(those ruptured concrete accretions
so tricky in winter),
where ever-overcast skies
feel fossilized, and memorization

appears far more practical
than invention. One day
he discovers he's named
for his father, though

loosely: a simple rearrangement
of those older monikers,
first and middle switched.
A name contrived by

a family overly fond
of checkers. Another time
he finds out that
his first name means

rock, which he interprets
as *solid* or *strong*,
but which others experience
most often as *stubborn*.

Never does he ask
anyone about the origin
of his bear's name.
It will remain always

that plain label rhyming
with his favorite dessert,
which, like himself, neither
hides nor reveals much.

Departure

He's lived two decades in this house.
Today's the day he has to leave.
It makes him want to have a drink
while he sits waiting for the sun
to light the branches of the elder.
His thoughts attempt to light the past.

Yet he knows dwelling on what's passed
this final morning in the house
is selfish. Staring at the elder
won't change the fact they have to leave,
or help console his wife and son.
He knows this. Still, he'd like a drink.

Just one, he thinks, *just a small drink*—
enough to help him make it past
this next hour when he's sure his son,
stomping through the empty house,
will scream, "Why do we have to leave?"
The boy reminds him of his elder

brother, who'd sit beneath the elder
with him each Saturday and drink
those anxious weeks he was on leave,
though since then twenty years have passed.
There was that phone call to the house
one August, just before his son

was born, but nothing more. The sun
spreads swiftly now between the elder
leaves as it climbs the waking house.
There's no time left for one last drink,
no time to clarify the past.
He'll tell his son, "It's time to leave,

that's why, because it's time to leave,"
and then turn in the glaring sun
as from a test he hasn't passed.
He'll never lean against the elder
again, enjoying a cold drink,
or sit here thinking in this house

about the past. Knowing both elder
and house are lost, he needs a drink.
But he, his wife, and son must leave.

Balance

He waited till dusk to try again.
The other kids had pedaled home,
leaving the treeless lane abandoned,

no sound of voice or car or siren.
At the corner, a streetlight stammered on,
moths skipping off its downward dome.

Earlier that summer his father
had joined him here, guiding the back
of his bike while shouting, "steady, steady!"

And then the fated letting go,
the widening wobble he couldn't control,
another spill on lawn or sidewalk,

the front wheel skewed (its fender warped
from previous falls), an elbow bruised,
his knee bleeding as he stood up.

"He's fine," he had heard the old man tell
his mother as he went outside.
"Some things you have to learn alone."

Reading Together

1981

My father reads out loud to me
from books I can't yet understand.
I'm four and balanced on his knee.
My father reads out loud. To me
it sounds like setting letters free—
as if they act at his command.
My father reads out loud to me
from books I can't yet understand.

2016

My father tries to read out loud
from books he once could comprehend.
His face perplexed, his bald head bowed,
my father tries to read out loud.
I slouch beside him, silent, cowed.
Here's something words will not transcend.
My father tries to read out loud
from books he once could comprehend.

The Quality of Small

after Les Murray

Small is
the quality
of that
coral-shorn
sea, his
memory, how
errant recollections
still register,
albeit infrequently—
bubbles sprung
from below
making nervous
surface dimples.
Small, this
sea receding,
no temporary
ebb. This
shallow sea
now everything.

Face Value

He used to guess who I might be—
his father or brother—the dead
resurfacing in my complexion.

"No," I'd say, "but close."
Then gently I'd correct him.
Today he struggles on in the silence

of his pinched gaze, like a child
attempting to read the board
from the back of the class.

Sometimes it seems he's just pretending,
on the edge of breaking
character in my presence.

At lunch, helping to feed him,
I study each shift in his expression,
seeking a breach in the mask, a tell:

a flinch, an eye-gleam, a keen glance held
one beat too long. Some slight yet pointed gesture
I'd recognize but never call as a bluff.

Then we could be conspirators,
which, like loss, bears its own coded burdens.

Caught

I catch myself speaking to you
as I would an infant or animal,

or speaking *of* you to the nurses
with you close by. This morning you nod

toward the constant loop of news
flashing from the dayroom wall.

I remember once you joked with me
that the media was made to get

seniors to scream and spend their savings.
You're long past that danger now.

When the program breaks for a commercial,
the television's volume surges,

just as an idling engine's revved
before it's shifted into gear.

Yet going where? No place for you
but back to bed, to the Neptune glow

of your own solitary screen . . .
May it dream for you that chambered glare

aimed at twin oncoming beams,
out along a highway's edge

where blacktop meets the trees—for you
that sudden, liberating leap.

Home Movies

What did you find,
those years behind
the camera's lens,
hidden from friends
and family,
no memory
left uncropped?

The films have stopped.
So why do I climb,
alone each time,
to the darkness of
this room above
my own loved ones:
a wife, two sons
you never met?

What will I get
from trying to
discover who
you really were,
departed blur?
Behind drawn drapes

I search old tapes;
their bland narration
of each vacation
and grainy hue

have outlived you—
who wouldn't relent
until an event
was captured by
your restless eye.

Photograph

Glimpsed from across the living room it seems
a normal portrait of an aging couple,
taken for their church directory,
framed and placed on a built-in shelf beside
a vase of red carnations and baby's breath.

Up close, though, something's off. Gone are the seams
on their cheeks and foreheads, yet the skin not supple,
just blank. An airbrushing—designed to free
this likeness from time's price—has been applied
to strange effect, forging not youth but death.

The Diver

At the hospital,
a hollow, pressurized
hiss, as from
a diver's mask,
marks his breath:
brief buoyancy, long
depth. Our task
is to watch
as he floats
too still, though
no one dares
to say it's
the last time
we'll see him
alive. No one
speaks. The diver
continues to dive.

False Elegy Beginning with the Moon

A blurred beam floated face down on the river—
crumpled, discarded, daylight's IOU.
From your darkened hospital room this was the view
that night the doctors gave you waning odds.
The priest gave you last rites, but it wasn't over,
your body defying medicine and God

to make a limited recovery.
You lived yet have kept little of what you called
your life, a garden still nearby but walled
off now from view. In your new home at the home,
you struggle with life's basics day-to-day,
needing help to brush your teeth or comb

your hair. Each evening, though, you phone to check
how my day's gone and, when the mundane has been
exhausted, pause, before you ask again
what happened during the weeks you were "knocked out,"
just as a child might question what life was like
before her birth, as if knowing what it's about

were a matter of attendance. I recount
those frequent visits to intensive care,
confirm that part of you remained aware,
squeezing my hand tightly when I spoke
your name. I've chosen not to add how gaunt
your cheeks looked, muscles slack as after a stroke,

or to mention your resemblance to that moon
so often dimmed yet not erased by day.
I wait for you to announce, "It's late." I say
"I love you." Answering, you add, "Good night."
After, my own gaze in the mirror seems wan—
holding fast to its brief and borrowed light.

Odd Elegy

She died on a day
gray and stippled
as an armadillo's shell.

Pines and firs
were drained of color,
the sky a murky brine.

Swaddled shoppers
tottered on the ice
in the parking lot of a mall,

averting their eyes
to escape the smart
of the wind, spines knuckled over

by cold. The only
green winked from wallets
or the salt-filmed sides of cars.

Sleeping in Your Parents' Bed

Tonight, gray-haired, you pull
back sheet and comforter,
curl up alone on your side.
It seems so small, this full-
sized mattress, much less wide
than you remember when
you last sought refuge here
from all a child could fear
in the dark. Your tired mind tries
to picture how they were,
who will never rest here again.
Lie still now. Close your eyes.

Lullaby for an Adult

after Patric Dickinson

All the doors are locked.
The dog's been walked.

Each tap, each burner off.
No dome-light glows in the garage.

Through that cracked blind
the streetlamp doubles

as your moon. You sleep alone
but this bed's warm.

Your dreams won't paralyze
or force contortions. Your face,

though pocked and stubbled,
softens. The ticking clock

has gone; your pulse
marks time, throbbing

through the splinter
burrowed in your palm.

No termite, no errant spark
will test these walls tonight.

Apology to Candles

Because we use you mostly
for show, personal or public:
a romantic dinner, birthdays, Mass.
Because for our everyday lives
you seem too decadent somehow
or dangerous, and prized more
for scent than your fragile,
fluent light. Because we stash
you in a drawer, unspoken
fears awaiting the next disaster.
Because we fail to recognize
that the shiver of filaments
within each incandescent bulb recalls
flames wavering on their wicks
when a draft passes through
the room. And yes, because
too often we place you
in a child's bewildered grip
at the latest neighborhood vigil,
your sputtering and fervid gestures
reminding us how shadows shift.

Late Inquiry

How did it end? What dealt the fatal blow?
Did it burn like a house with a faulty kitchen stove?
If we'd sifted the ashes, would we have found a clue?
No ashes now, just the syllables of doves.

Were there warning signs? Did they send a boy for water?
Not a soul is left to ask; everyone's gone.
And now that it's over, *how* seems not to matter.
The doves remain, ash-humble in the sun.

II

My friend says epigrams have an easy wit.
He would prefer that twitching bit by bit
Conceit of what he's never sure is it.

—John Finlay

Dial Tone

Seems strange to miss this barren baritone
once known to all—and by all overthrown—
to miss, whenever I pick up my phone
and make a call, the barely noticed drone
that spoke of reaching out, of being alone.

In Memory of Ray Dolby

He challenged noise and won,
rinsing the hiss from analog
recordings the way the sun,
on humid mornings, dissolves the fog.

Wind

Lubbock, TX

Sharpened vacancy.
    Shifting, angled sting
      smelling of dust or rain.
      Ubiquitous. Arcane.
Carries debris like a tune
in some gritty minor key,
    the horizon brown as a dune.
    Hums. But does not sing.

Hyperopia

Youth's hard to see, until we've seen it through.
Only old eyes can recognize what's new.

Deciduous

Because our movements hint at flight
some think that we resemble wings.
But we're unpaired, descending things,
impelled by gravity or blight.

Seasonal

When glaciers and ice caps abate,
when aerosols have hacked the atmosphere,
    when just two seasons survive
        (rainy and warm, dry and hot),
    when those of us alive,
        lucky or not,
  behold the weather's flattened fate
like rulers who've ignored a seer,
        autumn will still adorn our sight
        with distinct, unscathed angles of light.

Standardized

Numb hours of teaching to the test
and hours more of silent filling,
filling of bubbles. A bored unrest
of minds, compliant though not willing.

Malpractice

Mark 2:17

Of course one must be cleansed of mortal sin
in order to receive the Eucharist.
Yet what humane physician would insist
only the healed ingest his medicine?

Patient

He wasn't dead; nor was he tougher.
What hadn't killed him made him suffer.

Prognosis

The medicines have ceased to make her stronger;
she takes them to stay weak a little longer.

Fears

Which thought incites more trepidation:
That death will permanently sever
this living tissue from sensation?
Or consciousness might last forever?

Vanity

Look in thy glass, and tell the face thou viewest
Now is the time that face should form another.
—Shakespeare

No, no. No son was meant to be a mirror
for his parents to relive their wasted youth;
proximity to the young just brings you nearer
to what you've lost for good. And how uncouth
of you, an otherwise nice man, to make
your gift to the world also a gift to yourself.
So natural when you began, so fake
now, prisoner to the bottles on the shelf
of your medicine cabinet, and all for what?
Not your old mother's joy (her mind dry rot);
not for your pride (that smile more limp than strut).
Listen, we fall apart. With kids or not,
sooner or later, nothing is what will be,
after a life of shouting *me! me! me!*

Teacher's Lament

Despite my games, bright PowerPoints, and maps,
I see few faces, just the tops of heads.
They while away the time with swipes and taps,

necks bent toward glowing desk-tops, palms, and laps.
Perhaps some haven't slept or missed their meds.
Despite my games, bright PowerPoints, and maps,

I've lost my students to the latest apps.
We waste our days in class at loggerheads.
They while away the time with swipes and taps;

I chide and lecture till my lungs collapse.
Like winter flu the disaffection spreads,
despite my games. Bright PowerPoints and maps

don't interest them. The useless hours elapse.
Often, I wish they'd stay home in their beds.
They while away the time with swipes and taps,

until I reprimand them in ALL CAPS,
though not enough to rip their trance to threads.
Despite my games, bright PowerPoints, and maps,
they while away the time with swipes and taps.

The Viewer

It's difficult to get news from the News.
Yet still he watches: whether to amuse
himself, or bolster his own static views,
or—feeling righteous—even just to lose
his temper (as his father did with booze),
he's not sure, and no longer looks for clues.
Much like his car, his mind is set to CRUISE.

He tunes in every evening, mutely chews
his food, stares like the spectators at zoos,
and thinks, *Oh well. I've worked hard, paid my dues.*
Why try to fathom every stranger's blues?
Though no one asks, most days he would refuse
to walk a mile, even in his own shoes.

Collars

1.

He hates his collar: always creased and blue;
he wants a job where he can wear a tie.
Though still unsure of what else he could do,
he hates his collar: always creased and blue,
torn, stained by grease, by sweat. "That's it, I'm through,"
he mutters frequently each day—a lie
he hates. His collar always creased and blue,
he wants a job where he can wear a tie.

2.

He has a job where he must wear a tie;
he wishes his white collar weren't so tight.
Though moneywise he's more than getting by,
he has a job where he must wear a tie,
compelling all employees to comply
with policies he rarely feels are right.
He has a job where he must wear a tie;
he wishes his white collar weren't so tight.

My Mama's Schmaltz

It seemed she only laughed
or looked remotely happy
when recollecting tales
I found extremely sappy.

If I came home from school
and saw her sipping tea,
I knew the next half-hour
would not belong to me.

She'd gab about past trips,
trite trinkets she collected,
her face a tear-puffed smile;
yet I felt unaffected.

She'd gush about the time,
one anniversary,
my dad bought all the mums
from Gaertner's nursery.

Most stories would begin
with "Once, when I was pretty . . ."
But I, a selfish child,
was not disposed to pity.

Those tedious afternoons
I'd fidget at the table,
and she would share her life—
part memory, part fable.

III

Growing both ways at once,
Alive in the light, in the dark . . .

—Theodore Roethke

Early June, Mid-Michigan

Populus deltoides

Now cotton seeds clot
the park's gullied paths
like pliant sprigs of snow.

In Praise of Blank Cassettes

Their labels were emblazoned only
with the trademarks of their manufacturers:
Philips, *Maxell*, *Sony*, *Memorex*.

I filled in the rest myself, armchair creator,
backseat DJ waiting anxiously
beside the boom box in my room until

that song reclaimed the radio, fingers
pressing PLAY and RECORD in unison
as I prayed the on-air personality

wouldn't botch the ending with his prattle.
Experts routinely credit the telephone,
but mixtapes spelled the end of *my* love letters

(a blessing, since my young left-handed script—
half rigor mortis and half seismograph—
befuddled more frequently than it enamored).

While others prospered by the crafting of bold,
bubbled vowels and chiseled consonants,
by the precise folding of pages ripped

decisively from wide-ruled spiral notebooks,
it was in the compilation of brief tracks
(tunes which enticed, then pleaded) that I excelled,

those missives made of ballads snatched from the airwaves—
just as swallows were ensnared in nets for counting,
but released again into an evening breeze

where they soon warbled . . . so my ardent tapes
alighted shyly on the waiting palms
of Katie, Jennifer, and Monica.

Ground Level

On unrelenting cloudless days when nothing's left
to transform overhead, I lie down prone and still

beneath the black walnut's shade, my mind recasting
the lawn instead. It's harder than with cumulus
or stratus; you can't just spot a cow and call it quits.

Allelopathic roots poison the soil, thinning
the turf in places much like drought. But while there are fewer

choices in that culled herd, the sparseness makes grass easier
to observe: one thick, striated shiv slices my gaze,
like a toenail exposed at the edge of a bed . . . another blade,

flimsy, frays at its end, a shoelace stripped of its aglet . . .
From afternoon to evening my mind fixes and drifts,

keeping, like my body, the bearings of a child
as I shift from belly to side to elbow, staying longer
than planned, forgetting laundry and dishes, till dew has groomed

our yard haphazardly and wet, disheveled whiskers
chafe my wrists and ankles, making them itch like hives.

The Yellowjackets Speak

*Most homeowners consider yellowjackets a pest, but
their diet actually makes them an important part
of garden pest control.*
—www.pestworld.org

You recognized too late we were not bees
and, stung repeatedly too near our nest
in the garden you were certain you possessed,
immediately deemed us enemies.

Even just one disrupted barbecue
was more than you could handle. "Kill them now!"
you squealed in comic rage, making a vow
to see us dead, yet careful to eschew

the act by calling on professionals,
who showed up promptly in protective gear
and felt, it seemed, neither disgust nor fear,
just as you felt guiltless. No confessionals

were needed here. In fact, you looked empowered.
Your flowers, though, will slowly be devoured.

Peonies in July

By sunrise it's already so warm
that the dew has fled our lawn.
The vaulted walnut chitters on.
Up early to refill the birdbath,
I shuffle with the bucket's brimming weight

across the yard, spying the peonies,
their withered heads fused to stooping stems,
brown and brittle, as if burned.
In June they were immense red blossoms
protected by the ants.

But now each petal has fallen
alone, lost in the thirsty grass.
Little remains except these slight
singed leaves, still seamed with green—
still shaped like narrowed eyes.

The Two-Body Problem in Cyberspace

Each day our pixels pack their bags and travel
across that distance measured more in hours
than miles. My evening reaches toward your night.
It's clear and calm here; there, sporadic showers
spatter the windowpanes with their failed flight.
I want to describe how the leafed and needled dusk
crosses my lawn, though your manner now is brusque,
tinged with anger and exhaustion (which
I know too well myself). What good is a voice
when there's cooking and dishes, a dog to walk?
Yet these calls usually help. Sure, we might bitch
or pout, but just the other's background noise
is enough to soothe. Sometimes we sit and talk,
imagining one couch. This can't unravel.

Anesthetic

Dead loved ones visit my wife's dreams to calm her;
bad jokes inhabit mine. A case in point:
You know why I'm not clinically depressed?
I've never been to a clinic. Dumb, of course,
but true. Without insurance we can't afford it.
So I do something else instead. On the nights
I wake from scenes of mortifying punch lines,
I sneak down to my office in the basement,
passing the bathroom, kitchen, and the guest room
(which would've been our daughter's room by now),
and, sitting at the plywood desk below
the garden—bald, drooping black-eyed Susans
peering through the smudged and narrow window—
I put on Spotify, search for a song
I haven't heard before but think I'll like,
then listen to it for an hour or more,
until I've memorized the lyrics, and
the rhythms they arrive in, and the notes
assigned to them, measure after measure.
Often, I softly sing along. It's soothing,
to concentrate and croon so long my jaw
begins to ache the way it used to when,
as an anxious kid, I'd chew big wads of gum
until all flavor and all hue but gray
was drained, and that bite-riddled mass spit out.
In elementary school I was the first
to learn my times tables by heart. This seems
similar, an accomplishment of sorts,

and feels great for a while but soon wears off.
The peace it brings me—if that's what it is—
diminishes more quickly these past nights,
like a pain pill I've depended on too much,
to which my body has become immune.

Mourning Doves

Not the raven holding all
the bruised hues of night,
but day arriving once more,
a gray warble heard first
from the box elder's limbs,

soon perching on the ledge,
beaks briefly pecking rectangular panes,
and, getting no answer, departing,
the whistled stutter of wings
dopplering off again until tomorrow.

Most mornings throughout the year
I wake to these sounds,
alone in the narrow bed
where my great-grandfather lay
eight decades ago. An engineer

for the Pere Marquette who
worked long and shifting hours,
he'd often rest by himself
in this second-floor room,
his wife a light sleeper.

Just after dawn, those times
he was home, he'd rise
and place pinches of millet
outside the window. Then doves,
taking turns, would fly from

branches to sill and eat—
as their descendants still try
at that appointed hour, though
they (like me) will never
receive such nourishment first-hand.

Winter Palette

A chickadee perched on
a paper birch's branch—
pearl, slate, obsidian, ash.

Trace

The night you disappeared
from us, there were
not even trace amounts
of drugs or alcohol

in your blood. You
just misjudged your speed,
the angle of that
too-familiar country curve

on a gravel trace
you had driven often
and thought you understood . . .
To remember it now,

in this ruined future,
feels like tracing shapes,
intimate and faded, across
translucent paper, the original

submerged yet legible beneath
time's curling onionskin, fogged
by the accumulating years,
by each diminished diopter.

Sugar Beets

Driving the narrow
two-lane between
Saginaw and Lennon
in late autumn,
past fields frozen
in harvest furrows,
the road treated
against the evening's
forecast of sleet,
rock salt rattling
like gravel in
the wheel wells,
I see, on
my left, beneath
tall stadium lights,
the beet-receiving
station—last week
an empty lot—
where now jagged
pyramids, Aztec or
Incan, rise darkly
to stunted summits,
piled bodies gnarled
and cratered, still
caked with clods
and root hairs,
concealing latent sweetness,
soon to disappear
again, refined into

masses of granules
equally as anonymous
as those places
that change them:
Croswell and Caro,
Bay City, Sebewaing.

Stumbling

over rocks in a field   rocks unseen
beneath tall rampant grasses
a tangle of nettles stinging my arm bitter-numb

you just ahead of me as I ask
annoyed   what the hell are these rocks
not rocks   you answer   stones

twenty years ago now   since then
a gate's been added   a fresh demarcating fence
collecting the warp of weather

that day we took time to observe
with squint and fingertip
the various effacements stone sustains

each skewed or sunken marker worn
to a blankness no human touch can fashion

Gardeners

Enveloped by the noise
of tools—mower, trimmer,
leaf-blower, or backhoe—
each man labors alone,

lacquered with daylit sound,
glowing like the stained
and sainted windows nearby,
even when it's overcast.

Those afternoons that I
stride past the plots
and paths these three
maintain, they nod, wave

politely from their distance.
The digging and planting
continue here year-round,
governed by other seasons.

The Fenced Field

A dark mound lists and settles,
reclaimed by teething grass.

Below, the last wait has begun,
that interval between *root* and *rooted*.

In death, as in life, we have made things difficult.
Your remains remain preserved and sealed.

How long before the anchored cedar knocks
and gnaws at the hull of the concrete vault?

How soon until the groundwater
gains purchase, then entrance?

The slow pulse of the soil
will crack encasement and gasket—

this muffled rupture the one sure rapture.
Beneath the surface, every surface

will be opened and dispersed
by the earth's digesting undertow.

Constitutional

The morning sky
resembles our faded
tablecloth, azure once,

its linen long
paled with age,
use, and cleaning.

Walking, my arthritic
tendon aches, torn
and mended years

ago, though soon
its pain dissipates.
She detested exercise.

Among my daily
excursions only this
still feels routine,

making my way
along the outskirts
of a park

close to home,
alive beneath that
slowly renewing blue.

After

On the table
purple asters curl
in a vase,

despite the water
he gingerly adds.
Gold centers darken.

Each stem loosens
from that spray
her hands arranged.

The Book

There's one book in his house he hasn't read,
its pages yellowing, its cover dirty.
This book lies next to him each night in bed.

Keeping it close, he feels some hunger fed,
as when a calm voice whispers, "Don't be worried."
There's one book in his house he hasn't read

but clings to, like a skin he's scared to shed
(and won't, just yet, refusing to be hurried).
This book lies next to him each night. In bed

it's splayed across his chest, set near his head,
or nudging his shoulder as he wakes, still weary.
There's one book in his house he hasn't read;

most nights he dwells on that last fight instead,
parsing every phrase. Since she remarried,
this book lies next to him each night in bed,

the bed where once she lay, bent limbs outspread
and warm, where even sleep now leaves him harried.
There's one book in his house he hasn't read;
this book lies next to him each night in bed.

Gray Areas

The ever-obvious elephant
inhabiting this rented room
awakens when we do.

I squeeze your shoulder
just a moment longer
in dawn's gauzed light.

Exhaustion on your face.
The early sky already
a net of nimbostratus.

Wind blurs the river.
Implication and allusion divert
our words like bends

in a stream, coy
voice of yours all
log-bob and eddy.

The Question

Midway through
our back-and-forth
about where to eat,
you pause, taking
a breath like a crisp page
turning.
          "What if,"
you say, "someday,
I needed something
from you, to live? A kidney,
maybe? Would you?"

"Oh, we'd never be
a match," I say.
"I mean, you know, sometimes
not even family, like
not blood relatives even, and we—"

"No, I know," you say,
"it wouldn't work. It's not likely
ever to happen anyway.
But what if? That's all.
Could you just say it
for me?"
         Along my sleeve
your index finger traces a crease . . .

Daybreak on Lake Huron

after Melissa Stein

As we crouch here, naked
near the water's edge,

toes sickled in wet sand,
I think of last night,

how, while you slept,
I studied the scar

scrawled across your wrist—
the one concealed,

even in summer,
by a buttoned sleeve.

This same flourish
I've seen on checks

and contracts when you cross
the *t* in our last name.

Now it glows faintly
as that line separating

pre-dawn sky from lake:
like pewter first, then tin,

then the sudden empty white
of just-cut skin before

light starts to seep
and seep above the horizon.

And we swim.

Endnotes

p. 12: The title and concept for this poem originate with Les Murray's poem "The Quality of Sprawl."

p. 20: The title of this poem was inspired, in part, by Brian Brodeur's poem "False Elegy."

p. 24: The title of this poem was adapted from Patric Dickinson's poem "Lullaby for Adults."

p. 32: "In Memory of Ray Dolby" is for William Logan.

p. 41: "Fears" is for Timothy Steele.

p. 74: This poem incorporates and modifies two phrases ("as you slept" and "and we swam") from Melissa Stein's poem "Quarry."